'The ple
is twice
When you cheat
a cheat.'

JEAN DE LA FONTAINE
Born 1621, Champagne, France
Died 1695, Paris, France

La Fontaine wrote 230 fables between 1668 and 1694.
This selection is taken from *Selected Fables* translated
by James Michie, Penguin Classics, 2006.

LA FONTAINE IN PENGUIN CLASSICS
Selected Fables

JEAN DE LA FONTAINE

The World is Full of Foolish Men

Translated by
James Michie

PENGUIN BOOKS

PENGUIN CLASSICS

UK | USA | Canada | Ireland | Australia
India | New Zealand | South Africa

Penguin Classics is part of the Penguin Random House group of companies
whose addresses can be found at global.penguinrandomhouse.com.

This selection first published in Penguin Classics 2016
001

Translation copyright © James Michie, 1979

The moral right of the translator has been asserted

Set in 9/12.4 pt Baskerville 10 Pro
Typeset by Jouve (UK), Milton Keynes
Printed in Great Britain by Clays Ltd, St Ives plc

A CIP catalogue record for this book is available from the British Library

ISBN: 978–0–241–25040–2

www.greenpenguin.co.uk

Penguin Random House is committed to a
sustainable future for our business, our readers
and our planet. This book is made from Forest
Stewardship Council® certified paper.

Contents

The Cicada and the Ant

The Cicada and the Ant

The cicada, having chirped her song
       All summer long,
    Found herself bitterly deprived
    When the north wind arrived –
Not a mouthful of worm or fly.
      Whereupon in her want
She rushed round to her neighbour the ant
      And begged her to supply
Some crumbs on loan to keep body and soul together
Till next spring. 'On my word as an animal
    I swear,' she said, 'to repay
With interest before the harvest ends.'
Of the ant's few faults the minimal
      Is that she never lends.
'What were you doing during the hot weather?'
She asked the importunate insect.
        'With all respect,
      I was singing night and day
For the pleasure of anyone whom chance
      Sent my way.'
       'Singing, did you say?
I'm delighted to hear it. Now you can dance!'

The Rooster and the Fox

The Rooster and the Fox

A shrewd, wily old rooster
Was keeping look-out on a bough
When a fox, in the nicest voice he could muster,
Addressed him: 'Brother,
We are no longer at war with each other:
I've come to announce that it's peace now,
Total peace! Descend and accept my embrace.
But for goodness' sake
Don't keep me waiting – today I'm in a hurry,
With twenty different calls to make.
From now on you and your race
Can go about your business free of worry –
We shall treat you as brothers. Let us light
Jubilee bonfires tonight.
Meanwhile come and receive a fraternal kiss.'
'My friend,' the rooster replied, 'I couldn't have heard
Better or more welcome news than this.

Peace is a wonderful word,
And to me it's a double delight
To hear it from you. But wait!
I see two hounds – they must be envoys sent
Expressly to attend this great event.
They'll be here in a moment, to judge by their pace.
Then I'll get down and we can all four embrace.'
'Goodbye,' said the fox. 'I've a long day ahead.
We'll have to celebrate
Tomorrow, or the day after . . .'

Whereupon, sick
At the failure of his trick,
That gentleman hitched his trousers up and fled.
The old cock watched his panicky retreat
With silent laughter;
For the pleasure is twice as sweet
When you cheat a cheat.

The Hare and the Tortoise

It's no good simply travelling fast;
What counts is not starting late –
As you'll see from the story I'm going to relate.
The tortoise once challenged the hare:
'Do you see that tree over there?
Let's have a race. I'll bet you come last.'
　　　'Last indeed!'
Retorted the animal famous for speed.
'Granny, take a dose of hellebore for your sanity's sake.'
'Sane or mad, I stand by my bet.'
'Done!' And by the tree each put down their stake.
What it was or who they agreed
To have as umpire isn't our affair.
　　　'Ready, get set . . .'
There were only a few steps for our hare to take –
　　I mean the sort of bounds
That a hare makes when, startled by hounds,
He sends them to the devil with a stride
That eats up miles of level countryside.
　　　Having, as I say, time to spare
　　　For napping, or for nibbling,
Or for sniffing out which way the wind was blowing,
He waited for the tortoise to get going.
Off she went, puffing and straining
Like an old senator, hobbling
As fast as she could, a pitiful rate.
　　　Meanwhile the hare,

The Hare and the Tortoise

Considering such a victory too cheap
And the prize hardly worth gaining,
Made it a point of honour to start late.

> He had a little feed,
> And then a little sleep,

He thought of everything but the race to be run.
Then he saw the tortoise almost at the winning-post
And was off like a flash at last, with a giant leap.

> Too late! The tortoise had won.

'Well!' she exclaimed. 'Didn't I make good my boast?

> What use is all your speed?
> Absolutely none!

How much farther behind do you think you'd be
If you had a house to carry like me!'

The Bear and the Garden-lover

The Bear and the Garden-lover

A certain half-licked mountain bear
Confined by Fate to the remotest lair
    Of the woods, living at odds
With the world (just like Bellerophon,
The hero hated by the gods),
Was going mad; for it's well known
That creatures soon do when they're left alone.
    Talk is good,
Silence is better still, but both are bad
When people carry them too far.
No beast set foot in that wild neighbourhood,
So that at last (bears being what they are)
He became sick of his miserable existence.
While he was busy being sad,
All this time an old eccentric loner
Was living within walking distance
    And feeling just as bored.
He was a garden-lover who adored
The goddess Flora, and likewise Pomona.
It's all right cultivating fruit and flowers,
    But in between I'd recommend
The presence of a sober, sensitive friend.
Gardens don't talk, except in poetry books!
    And so, tired of long hours
Among his flower-folk with their speechless looks,
One fine morning he set off to find
Some company in the countryside.

At the same time, with the same thing in mind,
      The bear began to descend
From his mountain home, and by a freak of chance
The two met, coming round a bend.
        The man was terrified.
What should he do? Retreat? Stand still? Advance?
Since the best thing in such a case
Is to put on a brazen Gascon face,
He managed to disguise his fright.
The bear, not used to being polite,
Growled: 'Visit my lair.' The other replied.
'Noble sir, you can see my cottage.
Will you do me the honour of eating there?
It's a rustic meal – fruit, milk and pottage –
      Probably not the regular fare
      Of a most distinguished bear,
      But what I have is yours to share.'
        The bear consented.
On the way they soon became a cordial pair;
Once they arrived the friendship was cemented,
      For though as a general rule
It's better to live alone than with a fool,
Since most of the day his guest remained quite mute
The man was free to tend his flowers and fruit.
      Meanwhile the simple brute
Went off hunting and brought back game
Or else indulged his favourite pursuit
Of catching insects; often he would keep
Those wingéd pests ('flies' is the vulgar name)
From his friend's face when he dropped off to sleep.

One day a fly perched on the nose of the man
When he was sunk in dreams and drove the bear
For all his vaunted prowess to despair.
'I'll get you this time!' Done as soon as said.
The faithful swatter carried out his plan.
Hurling a paving-stone as hard as he could,
He crushed the fly – and with it his host's head.
Marksmanship excellent; thinking not so good,
Where a man had been, a corpse was stretched instead.

      An enemy with common sense
Is far less dangerous than a friend who's dense.

The Stag Who Saw Himself in the Water

The Stag Who Saw Himself in the Water

A stag, in the clear mirror of a stream,
Was considering his appearance. His self-esteem
Was gratified by his fine antlers, but his spindling
Shanks, whose image he saw dwindling
   Unimpressively away,
   Filled him with pained dismay.
Dolefully eyeing his reflection, he said:
'What disproportion between feet and head!
   My branched head overtops
   The branches of the highest copse,
   But my legs do me no credit.'
   Scarcely had he said it
Than a bloodhound appeared and forced him to make
A dash to the woods for safety's sake.
   There his antlers, those splendid
Ornaments, hindering every step, denied
The help his legs were eager to provide,
   Upon which his life depended.
Now he unsaid those words, regretting dearly
The gifts which Nature renewed on his brow yearly.

   What is beautiful we prize;
   What is merely useful we despise;
Yet what is beautiful is often our destruction.
The stag scorned the legs which lent him speed,
And cherished the horns which in his hour of need
   Were a dire obstruction.

The Peasant and the Snake

Aesop tells of a peasant with a kind
Heart but a rather simple mind
Who on a winter's day going the round
Of his acres noticed on the snowy ground
An adder numbed with cold, stiff as a board,
Bound in a matter of minutes to expire.
He picked the snake up and, returning
Home, with no thought of earning
Thanks for his good deed laid it by the fire.
Slowly the paralysed body thawed
Till life, with heat, came back to the creature,
And with new life its angry reptile nature.
At first it feebly reared its head and hissed,
Then coiled its length and tried to strike, but missed,
Its benefactor, foster-father, saviour.
'Ungrateful thing!' he cried. 'Is this my reward?
Die, then, for your behaviour!'
And in a righteous fury seized his axe
And with two mighty hacks
Made of the tail, the middle and the head
Three little snakes, all dead.
They writhed and squirmed to join themselves again,
        But writhed and squirmed in vain.

It's a fine thing to be kind, but it all depends:
Kind to whom? As for ingrates who turn on friends,
Sooner or later they come to sticky ends.

The Fox and the Grapes

A starving fox – a Gascon, Normans claim,
But Gascons say a Norman – saw a cluster
Of luscious-looking grapes of purplish lustre
Dangling above him on a trellis-frame.
He would have dearly liked them for his lunch,
But when he tried and failed to reach the bunch:
'Ah well, it's more than likely they're not sweet –
    Good only for green fools to eat!'

Wasn't he wise to say they were unripe
    Rather than whine and gripe?

The Frog Who Wanted to be as Big as the Ox

The Frog Who Wanted to be as Big as the Ox

A frog saw an ox: in his eyes
A huge and handsome figure.
He, who was no bigger
Than an egg from top to toe,
In envy stretched and strained in an effort to blow
Himself up to the same size.
'Just watch me closely, Sis.
Tell me, am I large enough?
Have I got there yet?' 'No.' More huff and puff.
'Well, look at me now!' Another 'No'.
'Then what about this?'
'You've still a long way to go.'
At which the poor frog, overloaded
With wind and vanity, exploded.

The world is full of men as foolish as that.
The tradesman wants to build like an aristocrat.
The petty prince employs
Ambassadors; the marquess errand-boys.

The Lion and the Rat

The Lion and the Rat

In this world we must do our best
    To oblige others; for we all
    Occasionally have need to call
On the services of the weak and small.
    This truth two fables attest:
Indeed proofs of all such truths abound.

Rashly popping from a hole in the ground,
A rat came up between a lion's paws.
The king of beasts, sheathing his claws,
In this instance showed his royal nature
    And spared the little creature.
The kindness wasn't wasted . . . But a rat
      Paying a lion back a debt –
      Could anyone credit that?
And yet it happened. On the fringe of the jungle
The same lion was later caught in a net
Which all his roars were powerless to untangle.
      Up ran Sir Rat and set
To work with his teeth, gnawing and fretting,
Till, mesh by mesh, he'd unpicked all the netting.

Patience and perseverance at length
Accomplish more than anger and brute strength.

The Oak and the Reed

The Oak and the Reed

One day the oak said to the reed:
'You have good cause indeed
To accuse Nature of being unkind.
To you a wren must seem
An intolerable burden, and the least puff of wind
That chances to wrinkle the face of the stream
Forces your head low; whereas I,
Huge as a Caucasian peak, defy
Not only the sun's glare, but the worst the weather can do.
What seems a breeze to me is a gale for you.
Had you been born in the lee of my leaf-sheltered ground,
You would have suffered less, I should have kept you warm;
But you reeds are usually found
On the moist borders of the kingdom of the storm.
It strikes me that to you Nature has been unfair.'
'Your pity,' the plant replied, 'springs from a kind heart.
But please don't be anxious on my part.
Your fear of the winds ought to be greater than mine.
I bend, but I never break. You, till now, have been able
    to bear
Their fearful buffets without flexing your spine.
But let us wait and see.' Even as he spoke,
From the horizon's nethermost gloom
The worst storm the north had ever bred in its womb
        Furiously awoke.

The tree stood firm, the reed began to bend.
The wind redoubled its efforts to blow –
   So much so
   That in the end
It uprooted the one that had touched the sky with its head,
But whose feet reached to the region of the dead.

The Town Rat and the Country Rat

Town Rat once graciously
Asked Country Rat to dine
On ortolans left over
By the household. On a fine

Turkish cloth the plates
And knives and forks were laid.
I leave you to imagine
How merry the two friends made.

It was a handsome spread,
All that a rat could wish.
Yet someone marred the mood
Half-way through the main dish.

Their ears picked up a sound
At the dining-room door. Cat!
Town Rat bolted for cover,
Followed by Country Rat.

The scratching ceased, the prowler
Moved off. At once the host
Led his friend back to the field:
'Now let's finish our roast.'

'That's enough, thanks,' said the other.
'Tomorrow you'll be my guest.
It's not that I'm critical of
The food – you served the best.

But at home I eat in peace,
And nobody interrupts.
Goodbye, then. And to hell
With pleasure that fear corrupts!'

The Frogs Who Asked for a King

The frog nation, becoming bored
With democracy, raised such a fractious cry
That Jupiter appointed them an overlord.
The king who came down was far from being harsh;
Yet he made such a noise when he fell from the sky
    That the people of the marsh
    Rushed to hide themselves in the pools,
    In the reeds and rushes, in every nook
    Of their froggy bog,
    Without for a long time daring to face
    This strange giant. In fact it was a log
That had made the awesome splash. The first frog
    Who was daring enough to take a look
    Quitted his hiding place
    And swam up, trembling in every limb.
Another followed the first, a third followed him,
    Until finally a whole swarm,
    Getting cheekier and bolder,
Actually hopped on their monarch's shoulder,
Without a murmur of protest from the inert form
Of the old chap. Before long the frogs were clamouring:
    'We want an active king!'
    By now nearly out of his mind
With annoyance, Jupiter sent them a crane,
Who breakfasted and lunched and dined
On frogs whenever he felt inclined.
And still the frogs continued to complain.

This time Jupiter told them flat:
'Don't be silly. Do you think that my decrees
Can be repealed just as frogs please?
To start with, you should have kept
Your own government. Failing to do that,
You should have been content to accept
Your first king, who was amiable and kind.
     Learn to be grateful
     For the one you have – or you may find
     The next king far more hateful.'

The Wolf and the Lamb

Might is right: the verdict goes to the strong.
To prove the point won't take me very long.

     A lamb was once drinking
From a clear stream when a foraging wolf came slinking
     Out of the woods, drawn to that quarter
     Of the countryside by hunger.
     'How dare you muddy my drinking water!'
     Said the beast of prey in anger.
'You shall be punished for your insolence.'
     'Your Majesty,' answered the lamb,
'I beg you not to be angry but to think
     Calmly about it. Here I am,
     Relieving my throat's dryness
At least twenty yards downstream from your Highness,
     And in consequence
     I cannot be in the least
     Guilty of sullying your royal drink.'
     'But you are,' said the pitiless beast.
'Besides, I know you spoke ill of me last year.'
'How could I have done? I wasn't even here,'
The lamb replied. 'I'm still at the teat of my mother.'
'If it wasn't you, it must have been your brother.'
'I haven't got one.' 'Well, then, one of you sheep;
For you and your shepherds and damned dogs keep

The Wolf and the Lamb

Making it harder and harder for me to eat.
But now revenge is mine – and revenge is sweet!'
Whereupon he dragged the lamb deep
Into the forest and had his meal.
There was no right of appeal.

The Lion in His Old Age

The lion, whom all the forest fears,
      Overburdened by years
And mourning his great prowess of the past,
      Was attacked at last
By his own subjects, who as he grew older
      Became bolder and bolder.
The horse approached and gave him a kick,
      The wolf a nip with his teeth,
      The ox a gore with his horn.
      The mortally sick,
      Miserable, age-worn
Lion could scarcely muster a roar
And uncomplainingly awaited death.
But when he saw the donkey at his door,
      He was moved to exclaim:
      'No, this is too much!
I'm ready to die, but to endure your touch
Would be to die a second death – of shame!'

The Lion in His Old Age

Women and Secrets

A secret is the heaviest load:
To carry one even a few steps down the road
Is hard for a woman; and many men – I speak
With experience – are femininely weak.

One night a husband, to test his bride
Beside him in the darkness, suddenly cried:
'Good God! What's happening? I can't bear it! My flesh
Is being torn apart! Merciful heaven,
    I'm giving . . . aaah, I've given
    Birth to an egg!' 'An egg?'
        'Yes, there it is, right by my leg,
        Absolutely fresh.
But don't tell anyone, in fact not a single word,
Or people will go round calling me a bird.'
        Knowing little of life
And still less of a case like this, the young wife
        Believed it and solemnly swore
To keep her lips sealed, then and for evermore.
        But with the shadows of the night
        That promise faded away.
Being indiscreet and not too bright,
She jumps out of bed at the peep of day
And runs round to her neighbour:
'Mother, the strangest thing has just occurred –
        But please don't breathe a word
        Or you'll get me a beating.

Last night my husband went into labour
And produced an egg as big as *that*.
This is a secret strictly not for repeating,
In God's name keep it under your hat.'
'Don't be silly,' says the other. 'Ah, my dear,
You don't know me. Go home. Have no fear.'
While the egg-layer's wife was returning,
The old biddy, of course, was burning
To be the first with the news. Off she races
And spreads it in a dozen different places.
   Her version adds two eggs more.
   Worse follows: another crone
   Whispers in someone's ear – an act
By now of supernumerary discretion –
   That she knows for a fact
   That the number was four.
From mouth to mouth, by rumorous progression,
By the end of the day the total has grown
   To well above five score.

The Dairymaid and the Milk-can

With a milk-can on her head
Set firmly on a pad,
Here comes Perrette,
Hoping to walk to town without an upset.
Short-skirted and lightly clad,
She strides along with a quick tread,
Having today, for greater ease,
Put on flat-heeled shoes and a plain chemise.
Already our dairymaid
Is lost in a waking dream
Of all the money she's going to be paid
For the milk she'll sell at the fair,
And afterwards how she'll spend it there:
She'll buy a hundred eggs and breed
Three times as many chicks. With work and care,
She tells herself, the scheme
Is certain to succeed.
'It won't be very hard
To raise the chicks in my back-yard;
The fox will have to be extra stealthy
Not to leave me enough to purchase a pig,
To fatten the pig won't cost me much in feed
(I must have bought him reasonably big),
And when I sell him I'll be really wealthy!
Then, with the proceeds, what's to stop
Me fitting up our stable for a cow,
And her calf too? I can see it now

            In my mind's eye
Skipping and frisking with the herd . . . '
            Here, suiting deed to word,
            Perrette gave a rapturous hop –
            And lost her balance and her load.
Chickens and pig and cow and calf, goodbye!
            Her fortune spilt on the road,
            The owner of all that stock
            With a woebegone expression
Went home to her husband to make her confession.
            I expect he gave her a knock.
So ends my farcical recital,
Which has 'The Milk-can' for a title.

Who doesn't build castles in Spain?
Which of us isn't mildly insane?
Picrochole, Pyrrhus, the dairymaid,
Wise men and fools alike, we all daydream
            (No pleasure in life is so sweet)
            And each of us is betrayed
            By flattering self-deceit –
The world's riches and honours seem
Ours then, and all its lovely women at our feet.
            Whenever I'm alone
My imagination rambles, I browbeat
Heroes, topple the great Shah from his throne,
The adoring populace hail me instead
And diadems are showered on my head –
Until some little mishap ends my reign
            And I'm my old fat self again.

The Tortoise and the Two Ducks

The Tortoise and the Two Ducks

A simple-minded tortoise,
Tired of living curled
In her hole, conceived a desire to see the world.
It's easy to glamorize foreign places;
Lame folk get to hate their own cramped quarters.
Two ducks, to whom the dear old Gran
Confided her ambition, at once proposed a plan
To help her: 'Do you see that great route up there?
We'll take you along it to America, by air.
You'll see all sorts of kingdoms, republics, races;
The different customs you'll observe will broaden your mind.
Why, Ulysses did the same.'
Although she'd hardly expected the hero's name
To be introduced here,
The tortoise liked the idea
And a deal was made. Soon the birds had designed
A machine by which the voyager could ascend.
Jamming a stick in her mouth crosswise
And telling her: 'Bite hard! Don't let go!'
Each of them gripped it at one end.
Up went the tortoise, and the world rubbed its eyes
To see the proverbially slow,
House-bound creature soaring with a duck on either side.
'A miracle!' somebody cried.
'Come and look at the queen of the tortoises sailing the
    skies!'
'The queen! Why, yes, that's exactly who I am –

And don't let anyone scoff!'
    She would have been far better off
To have made her flight in silence like a clam,
    For, unclenching her teeth,
She dropped the stick, fell and was smashed to bits at the feet
    Of the gazers beneath,
    Her folly the cause of her death.

    Garrulousness, inanity,
    Inquisitiveness and vanity,
All spring from one parent seed,
Are all children of the same narrow breed.

The Little Fish and the Angler

A little fish will grow,
Providing that God gives it time to, fatter;
    But to let a tiddler go
And wait for that to happen in my view
    Is a silly thing to do.
To catch fish twice isn't a simple matter.

One day a carp, still very young and small,
Was caught by an angler on the riverside.
'Well,' said the man, examining his haul,
'Everything counts. There's a delicious meal
Building up here. We'll pop it in our creel.'
The poor carp in his squeaky fashion cried:
'What are you going to do with me? For you
Half a mouthful's all I can provide.
    Let me grow up, and by and by
    I'll see to it that I'm caught
By you again, and then I'm sure to be bought
By some greedy tax-man from the Revenue
For a good price. If not, you'll have to try
    To catch a hundred other fish
    Of my size to make up a dish.
Some dish! Trust me, it'll be a paltry feast.'
    'Paltry? So be it,' said the man.
'My fine and fishy friend, though you can preach
    As well as any priest,

For all your powers of speech
Tonight you end up in my frying-pan.'

A bird in the hand is reckoned
Worth two that you haven't yet shot.
The first bag's certain, the second
        Is not.

The Farmer and His Sons

Hard work, taking trouble –
There you have capital that's sure to double.

A rich farmer, feeling the onset of death,
Summoned his sons for a talk in private.
'Never,' he said with his remaining breath,
'Sell the heritage that is yours by birth
And was mine through my father and mother.
      Somewhere or other
A treasure lies hidden in that earth;
Where, I don't know, but in the end you'll arrive at
The right place, given some guts and toil.
When you've finished harvesting turn over your land,
Break it up, dig it, plough it, don't allow
One inch of it to escape your hand.'
The old man died, and the sons attacked the soil
So thoroughly with spade, mattock and plough
That at the year's end every field
      Gave them a bigger yield.
They never found that buried hoard;
And yet their father was no fool.
Before he died he taught the golden rule:
      Work is the hidden reward.

The Doctors

The Doctors

Dr It-can't-be-helped and Dr It-can
Met at the bedside of an ailing man.
The latter – though his colleague's grim prognosis
Was that the sufferer would soon be seeing
His ancestors – took a more hopeful view.
        Opinions disagreeing
As to medicaments and doses
And Dr It-can't-be-helped's having prevailed,
        Their patient failed
And paid mortality its due.

And so, considered either way,
Medical knowledge won the day.
'There,' said the first, 'he's dead –
Exactly as I prophesied!'
'If he'd trusted me,' the other replied,
'He'd still have years of life ahead.'

The Hen Who Laid Golden Eggs

When greed attempts to win all, greed
Loses all. In support I only need
Cite the old story we've all heard
Of the man who owned a hen that used to lay
        A gold egg every day.
Convinced her gizzard was a treasure-vault,
He killed and opened up the bird,
Only to find an average specimen
        Of egg-producing hen.
        Thus he destroyed
        Through his own fault
The great bonanza he'd enjoyed.

For grabbers here's a pretty warning.
In recent years it's been a common sight
To see men ruined overnight
Who tried to make a fortune before morning.

The Dog Who Dropped the Substance
for the Shadow

Everyone under the sun
Deceives himself: so many madmen run
After shadows that one's half the time unable
To reckon their number up.
We must refer them to the fable
In which Aesop speaks of the foolish pup.

This young dog, carrying a dead rabbit
And seeing its reflection in a stream,
Opened his jaws, tried to grab it,
And was almost drowned
When the river suddenly turned choppy.
He just managed to regain dry ground –
Without either substance or dream,
Original or copy.

The Rat Who Retired from the World

The Rat Who Retired from the World

Here's an old story the Levantines tell.
A rat, weary of the troubles of this world,
Retired into a Dutch cheese. Profound
Was the global silence stretching all around
      Our new hermit curled,
       Far from care, in his nourishing cell.
     Within days his teeth and feet
Had gnawed and dug so deep that his retreat
Offered not merely board but bed as well.
What more was there to do? He grew sleek and fat –
      For God most generously endows
      Those who take other-worldly vows.
      One day our devout rat
      Was visited by a deputation
Of rats on their way abroad in search of aid
      Towards raising the blockade
      Of Ratopolis by the cat nation.
Due to the poverty of their hard-pressed city
They'd had to leave with nothing in the kitty
For travelling expenses. 'A small sum
Is all we ask. Fellow-citizen, take pity!
In a week at the most rescue is sure to come.'
      'Friends,' said the anchorite,
'I no longer concern myself with this world's affairs.
      How can a poor recluse
      Be of any use
To you here, except by offering up prayers?'

Heaven help you in your plight!
May God grant you His merciful grace!'
So saying, he shut the door in their face.

Whom do you think I'm pointing at
In the figure of the ungenerous rat?
    A Christian father?
    A heathen dervish rather!
For monks unfailingly relieve
Distress – at least so I believe.

A Fool and a Wise Man

A wise man, walking alone,
Was being bothered by a fool throwing stones at his head.
    Turning to face him, he said:
    'My dear chap, well thrown!
    Please accept these few francs.
You've worked hard enough to get more than mere thanks.
    Every effort deserves its reward.
But see that man over there? He can afford
    More than I can.
Present him with some of your stones: they'll earn a good
    wage.'
    Lured by the bait, the stupid man
    Ran off to repeat the outrage
    On the other worthy citizen.
This time he wasn't paid in money for his stones.
    Up rushed serving-men,
And seized him and thrashed him and broke all his bones.

In the courts of kings there are pests like this, devoid of
    sense:
They'll make their master laugh at your expense.
To silence their cackle, should you hand out rough
Punishment? Maybe you're not strong enough.
    Better persuade them to attack
Somebody else, who can more than pay them back.

The Oyster and the Litigants

One day two travellers, walking side by side,
Came on an oyster washed up by the tide.
Greedily they devoured it with their eyes,
Excitedly they pointed out its size,
And then, inevitably, they faced
The problem: which of them as judge
Should pass a verdict on the taste?
One was already stooping for the prize
When his friend gave him a nudge:
    'We must decide this properly.
    The epicure's monopoly
Belongs to whoever saw it first: *he* swallows
The oyster and, it logically follows,
    The other has to watch him do it.'
    'If that's the way you view it,
I have, thank God, remarkably keen sight.'
    'Mine's pretty good as well,
    And upon my life I swear
I saw it before you!' 'So what? All right,
    You may have been
The first to *see*, but I was the first to *smell*.'
Who should arrive upon this charming scene
But Perrin Dandin? Asked to intervene
    As arbiter in the affair,
    With a portentous air
    He digs the oyster from its shell
And gulps it while his audience stands and stares.

The meal finished, he declares
In the tone of voice beloved of presidents:
    'The court hereby decrees
An award, without costs, of one shell to each.
    Both parties please
    Proceed without a breach
Of the peace to your lawful residence.'

Count what it costs these days to go to court,
And how little the families driven to that resort
Have left after expenses. It's the Law,
It's Perrin Dandin who eats up the rest –
    Who takes the wing and breast
And leaves the litigants the beak and claw.